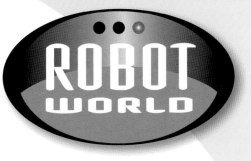

ROBOT WORLD

Robots in Science and Medicine

by Steve Parker

amicus

Published by Amicus
P.O. Box 1329
Mankato, MN 56002

Printed in the United States of America, at
Corporate Graphics in North Mankato, Minnesota.

Library of Congress Cataloging-in-Publication Data
Parker, Steve, 1952-
   Robots in science and medicine /
   by Steve Parker.
        p. cm. – (Robot world)
   Summary: "Discusses the latest advancements in
robotics and how they are used in scientific
research and in medical applications"–Provided by
publisher.
   Includes index.
   ISBN 978-1-60753-074-9 (lib. bdg.)
   1. Robotics–Juvenile literature. 2. Robotic in
medicine–Juvenile literature. 3. Robotics–Human
factors–Juvenile literature. I. Title.
   TJ211.2.P37 2011
   629.8'92–dc22

                                    2009040656

Created by Appleseed Editions Ltd.
Designed by Guy Callaby
Edited by Mary-Jane Wilkins
Picture research by Su Alexander

Picture acknowledgements
title Getty Images; contents Reuters/Corbis; 4 Pasquale
Sorrentino/Science Photo Library; 5 Charles O'Rear/Corbis;
6 STR/AFP/Getty Images; 7 Reuters/Corbis; 8 Sam Ogden/
Science Photo Library; 9t Sciencephotos/Alamy, b Issei Kato/
Reuters/Corbis; 10 Lester Lefkowitz/Corbis; 11 Judith Wagner/
Zefa/Corbis; 12-13 Peter Ginter/Science Faction/Corbis;
13 Karen Kasmauski/Corbis; 14t A .T .Willett/Alamy, b Time
& Life Pictures/Getty Images; 15 Indo Wagner/epa/Corbis;
16 Sam Ogden/Science Photo Library; 17 Photolibrary Group;
18 Phototake Inc./Alamy; 19 Getty Images; 20 George
Steinmetz/Corbis; 21t © Ossur, b Photo courtesy of METI,
© METI 2009; 22 Pascal Goetgheluck/Science Photo Library;
23 Robotic Systems & Technologies, Inc; 24 Reuters/Corbis;
25 Getty Images; 26 Makoto Iwafuji/Master Photo Syndication/
Sygma/Corbis; 27t AFP/Getty Images, b Volker Steger/Science
Photo Library; 28 Chistian Darkin/Science Photo Library;
29t Photolibrary Group, b Simon Fraser/Science Photo Library
Front cover: Peter Menzel/Science Photo Library

DAD0040
32010

9 8 7 6 5 4 3 2 1

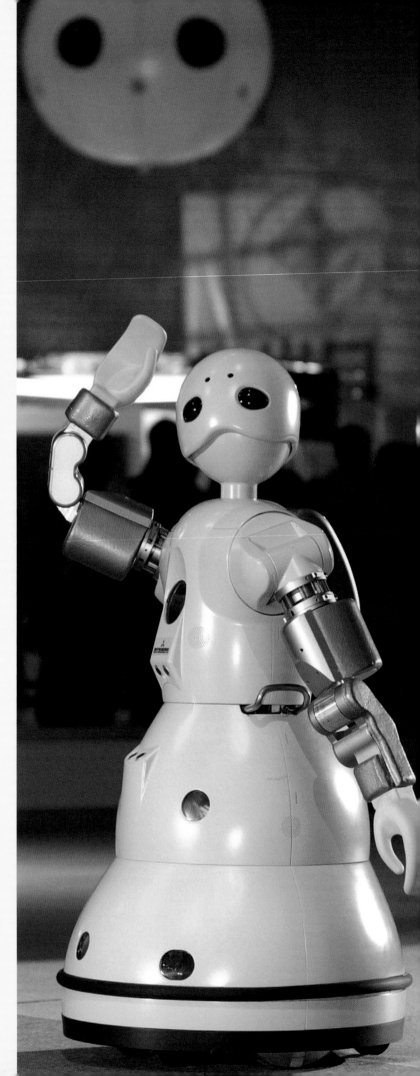

Contents

The Science Behind Robots

Without science, we would have no robots. People who make robots need to be experts in many areas of science, from mechanics, engineering, and physics, to math, **electronics,** and computers. Most robots are designed and built by teams of scientists. But what is a robot?

Engineers in Italy take off Babybot's head to reveal wires, cameras for eyes, and microphones for ears. Under the cute baby face is a lot of complicated science.

ROBOT OR NOT?
○ ○ ○

Must Robots Move?

Most robots have moving parts. But do robots have to move around on legs, wheels, or tracks? No. Many robots in factories are fixed in one place. They can reach out, lift, squeeze, push, and pull. But they can't walk, run, slide, or roll—they don't have to.

Robot Features

Most robots have moving parts, such as levers, gears, and motors. They are programmable, which means we tell them what to do. But they are also **automatic** and work on their own, to some extent, after they are programmed. Many robots can detect what happens around them, and alter their actions when needed.

Skeleton and Muscles

Robots have a framework or skeleton to support them and hold their smaller parts. This is usually made of metal or strong plastic. The frames of humanoid robots are inside, like the bones in your body. For hard-working factory robots, the frame can be outside, as it doesn't really matter what they look like.

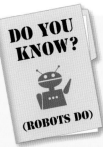
Robots Don't Know Faces

Even robots with the cleverest programming can't see as well as humans. It's difficult for a robot to recognize common objects by sight using its camera "eye," as we do all the time. This is known as pattern recognition. Humans can tell apart hundreds of faces at a glance. A robot has trouble with just a few.

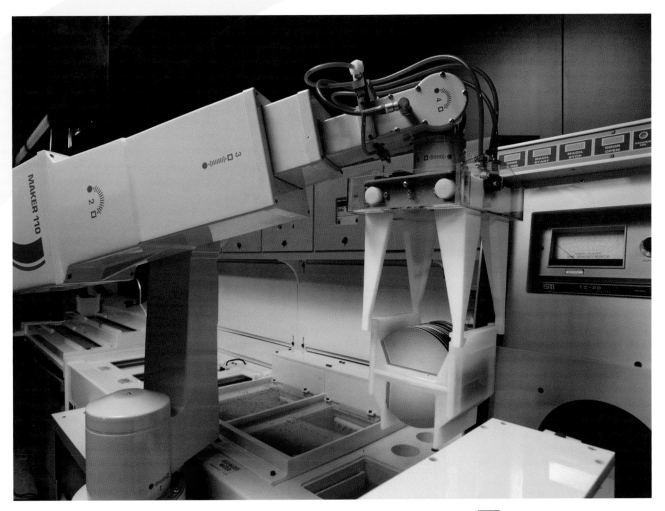

All day, every day, millions of robots do important factory jobs with their body parts. This one uses its swivel-waist, telescope-arm, and grab-hand to move thin sheets of silicon, which will become computer microchips.

Robots have motors that move their parts and act as "muscles." Usually these are electric motors, called servo motors or stepper motors, that move very precisely. Some motors power pumps for robot parts worked by high-pressure oil or air, which are called pneumatic or **hydraulic systems**.

Grip and Control

Many robots have grippers, suckers, claws, or clamps to hold and move objects. All robots have some kind of control system, usually **microchips** or a computer as a built-in "brain." There are also controls for people to program or teach the robot how to do its tasks.

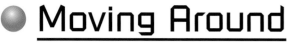 Moving Around

Robots don't move in the same way as humans, by locomotion. Those which do move have lots of ways of getting around. They can roll on wheels or balls, crawl on tracks, swim, fly, and even somersault. Strangely, the movement they find hardest is the one we find easiest—walking.

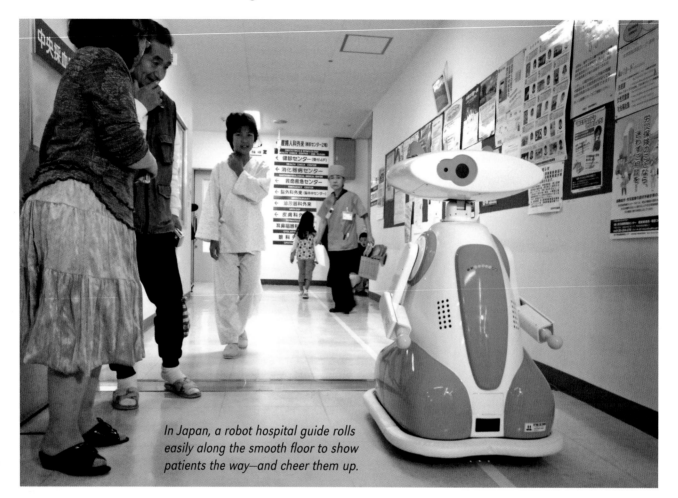

In Japan, a robot hospital guide rolls easily along the smooth floor to show patients the way—and cheer them up.

Robots in Action■

SIGN LANGUAGE

There are many ways to instruct a robot, such as using a computer keyboard and mouse, or speaking words. Some advanced robots have cameras that watch a person making gestures, like waving or nodding, as a form of sign language. The robot's computer works out what the person's gestures mean and the robot obeys.■

Rolling Around

Wheels are great for helping robots to get around. Many robots have them, usually between three and six. Some are designed so that each wheel is powered by its own electric motor. The robot turns a corner by making the wheels on one side turn faster than those on the other side. Other robots have wheels that swivel left or right, like the wheels of a car.

The problem with wheels is that they only work on fairly flat surfaces. They have trouble with rough ground, steep slopes, and stairs. Crawler tracks can cope with some holes and bumps, but they are slow and use lots of battery power. Another robot design has sets of three wheels instead of one, as in carts that can climb stairs. The wheels rock over bumps and pivot up steps.

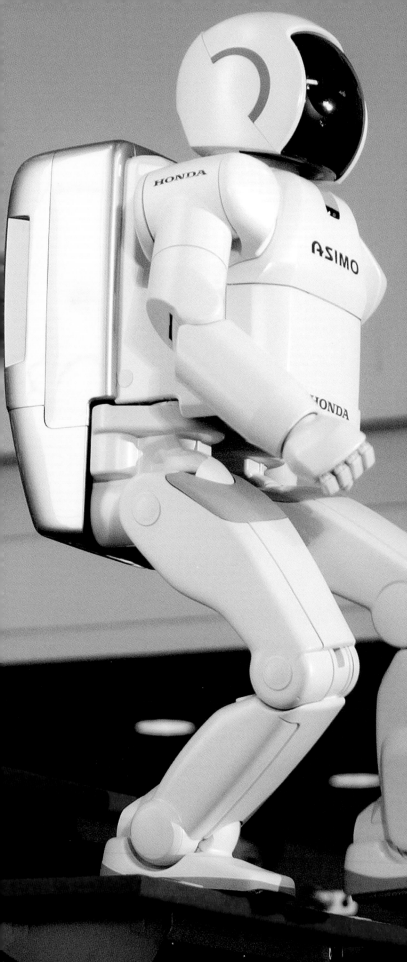

Walking

Humans are among the very few animals that usually walk upright. Designing a robot that walks has been a huge challenge, because a two-legged robot is naturally unstable and falls over. If they are given better balance **sensors** and quicker-acting electric motors, robots can react faster so they don't fall over.

ROBOT SUPERSTAR

Asimo

The human-shaped Asimo robots were built to study the problems of machines walking upright and keeping their balance. The first Asimo was made in 2000. The latest version is 4 feet 3 inches (130 cm) tall and can not only walk, but also run at about 5 feet (1.5 m) per second.

Robot Senses

Some robots seem to ignore what is happening around them, because they have no sensors or detectors, such as a camera to "see," a microphone to pick up sounds, or a pressure pad for touch. But scientists are experimenting with ways to program robots to "sense" their surroundings.

Seeing the Invisible

*Robot cameras can pick up kinds of light that our eyes cannot, such as IR (**infrared**) and UV (**ultraviolet**). IR light rays carry heat energy and are, in effect, heat rays. Future firefighting robots might "see" heat from a fire, warn us of the danger, and then go off to tackle the blaze.*

▶▶ *The robot android Cog has not two eyes, but four—two give a close-up view and two show the wider scene.*

Cameras to See

Human eyes work like living cameras to detect light and send the information to the brain. Lots of robots have cameras that look around. Most of them use a microchip called a **CCD** (charge-coupled device). It changes the patterns of light rays to patterns of **digital** electronic signals for the robot's onboard computer to analyze. For example, if an object gets bigger in the camera's view, the computer interprets this as meaning that the object is coming nearer.

Microphones to Hear

A microphone changes sound waves into digital electronic signals for the robot's computer. One of its main uses is for voice control. The computer compares the wave pattern of a sound it hears with the wave patterns in its memory, and picks the closest match, to identify commands such as "Stop" or "Go."

Shhh!

*Our ears are very good at picking up quiet sounds, but not as good as some robots' hearing. Their microphones are so sensitive that they can detect sounds quieter than 10 dB (**decibels**), which we cannot. This is useful in remote places to hear planes going overhead, or to alert workers on roads and railroads when trucks or trains are approaching.*

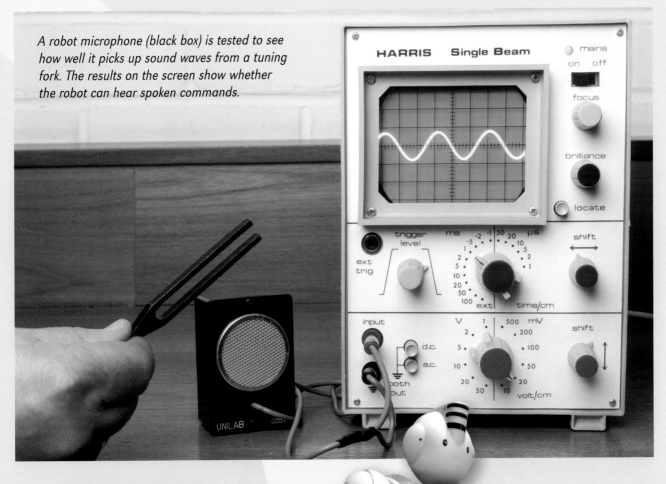

A robot microphone (black box) is tested to see how well it picks up sound waves from a tuning fork. The results on the screen show whether the robot can hear spoken commands.

Pressure Pads to Feel

Many robots can sense physical contact. In factories, robots have touch bars or **pressure pads**. As soon as these contact something, it means the robot is off course, or there is something in the way that shouldn't be there. The robot stops at once to avoid a crash.

◀◀ *Hitachi's Chum rolls faster than you can walk. Touch sensors on its head, waist, and near the wheels make sure it doesn't bump into things.*

How Smart Are Robots?

Robots can be programmed for one simple job, such as painting cars. Or they can have very complex programming that allows them to repsond to their environment. Fairly "smart" robots have computers the size of a laptop, and really intelligent ones have "brains" bigger than suitcases. To save space and weight, these computers are very unusual.

Specially Made
A robot's computer is not usually like the laptop or desktop computers that we use. It is tailor-made for the tasks that the robot is designed to do. This means that electronics engineers design and build the microchips and **circuits**, and computer programmers write special applications or software.

◄◄ *Developing a new robot means testing various hand-built circuits, each with dozens of components. When it all works properly, these can be reduced to one small factory-made version.*

AI, or **artificial intelligence**, is the science and engineering of making intelligent or clever machines. AI experts are always looking for ways to improve robot computers. In particular, they develop mathematical sums and **formulas** called **algorithms**. These help the computer to do such things as scan a scene in its camera and recognize which objects are there. Once it has done this, the computer can use more algorithms to decide how the robot should respond.

A Name to Match

What effect does a robot's appearance affect how clever or stupid we think it is? Does giving it a name rather than a number have any effect? In a way, yes. If a toy robot dog has no outer cover and is called XP-112-A, people often view it as just another dumb machine. If the same robot has a furry outer covering and big eyes, and is called Rover the Robo-puppy, we tend to react by thinking it is clever, as well as cute.

ROBO-FUTURE

Thinking Robots?

Will robots ever be able to think like humans? Every year, the Loebner Prize for Artificial Intelligence is awarded to the programmer of the most human-like computer at the Loebner contest. The 2009 winner was Dr. David Levy for his "Do-Much More" chatbot.

 *Designers make robot pets look appealing in many ways, for example, by adding floppy ears!*

Robot Television?

Is a television set a robot? It carries out a job—showing TV channels—and we can program it to switch on and off and record. But it does not make any movements or decisions itself, or sense and adapt to its surroundings. It is just a remote-controlled electronic gadget.

Robots in the Lab

Science laboratories are natural homes for robots. These are the places where many new types are built, tested, mended, and improved. Many working robots spend their days and nights in laboratories, carrying out research and scientific tests for their masters.

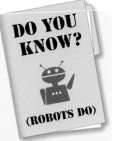

DO YOU KNOW?

(ROBOTS DO)

That's Secret!

Mass-produced robots are big business. So robot manufacturers don't tell everyone about the new models they are working on in the lab. They keep them secret, otherwise another robot-maker might try to copy and sell them, so the original inventor would lose lots of money.

```
Robots in Action■

PRETEND PERSON

Crash-test robots are pretend "human bodies"
fitted with many types of sensors to measure
the effects of vehicle accidents. These vary
from head-on impacts to being hit from the
side to what happens if a car plunges into
water. These robots are regularly repaired
with new parts to replace old, broken ones.■
```

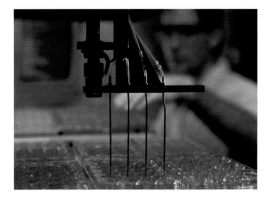

In a medical laboratory, a robot arm dips four narrow tubes into samples of liquids, to suck out exactly measured amounts. It does this roughly once every three seconds.

Testing, Testing

Every part of a robot needs to be tested to make sure that it can stand up to wear and tear and unusual conditions. A robot designed to go outside, for example moving across a factory yard, has to be waterproof and cope with hot sun or icy winds. So a test version of the robot is left out in all weather, or even sprayed with a hose to make sure that it can withstand rain.

Breakdown

Robots in factories have to work for many hours without breaking down or wearing out. When they are out of action, the factory loses money. So their motors, levers, gears, joints, and grabs are all tested to destruction, which means until they break. This is often done on machines called test rigs where the parts are pulled, twisted, and worked hard. If a bearing seizes up, mechanical engineers try to find out why. If a plastic part snaps, materials scientists find a stronger one.

Robot Teachers

Young scientists who want to become robot experts go to teaching laboratories. Here they study how to design and build robots and other machines. They take exams in subjects such as **robotics**, systems engineering, and artificial intelligence.

An engineer checks the wrist joint of a crash-test dummy before its next ride to disaster. These robots have helped prevent countless human injuries and deaths.

13

Sports Science and Robots

hen science meets sports, robots get involved. Some help players and athletes to train and improve their skills. Others test new designs and materials for sports equipment, from golf clubs and tennis racquets to bowling balls and snowboards. These robot testers take their equipment to the limit and beyond.

▶▶ *No matter how good human players are, they cannot throw the ball in exactly the same way every time, as a robot pitcher does.*

Let's Play Ball!
Ball-hurling robots are used in sports as varied as baseball, tennis, table tennis, volleyball, and football. They can throw and spin the ball as well as any world class player—fast or slow, near or far, time after time, without ever tiring.

A Good Kicking
Robot kickers are great training aids for soccer, rugby, and similar games. The swinging boot hits the ball within one millimeter of the same place every time. Robot kickers are programmed to copy the style of famous players, so that opponents can practice moves against them. Or they can be set to random so the ball flies out at a different speed and angle each time. This keeps the players on their toes.

The Same Every Time
The exact curve of a football, the size of the dimples on a golf ball, or the thickness of fibers on a tennis ball affect the way the ball flies through the air. A robot throws or kicks balls of different designs and materials exactly the same every time, to make comparisons. Baseball bats or tennis racquet strings can be made from different materials, and again a robot compares them.

ROBOT SUPERSTAR

Joe the Pitcher
One of the first sports robots was a baseball pitcher called Overhand Joe, made during the 1940s. It was a table-sized metal box with a whirling arm. Joe threw a ball every nine seconds and could be adjusted for direction, speed, and spin. He never tired or complained!

Robots in Action

ROBO-ATHLETES

Every year robot experts around the world send teams to play in the Soccer RoboCup. Robot makers test the latest sensors, motors, controllers, and other equipment. The goal is for a team of intelligent, human-shaped robots to beat a team of human soccer players by the year 2050.

Robots in Nature

Natural-looking robots disguised as animals, plants, or rocks can perform all kinds of special tasks in the wild. They observe rare creatures, spy on poachers who break the law by killing animals, and even pretend to be lumps of dung!

ROBOT SUPERSTAR

Roboshark

Several robot sharks have been built to swim alongside real sharks, in aquariums as well as in the ocean. Roboshark 2 is 6.5 feet (2 m) long and looks like a gray reef shark. It can be programmed to swim at various speeds and depths with four hours of battery power. Experts study how other sharks react to it and how fish behave when it comes near, ready to attack!

▶▶ *Robotuna has six electric motors and swishes its tail to move along. The test equipment measures its speed and power, to help scientists understand how fish swim so fast.*

Robots in Disguise

Many animals are nervous when people are nearby. They try to escape and do not behave naturally. But animals soon grow used to a robot, which has no smell or worrying movements. Robot cameras can observe them and move around to record the best pictures and sounds without disturbing them.

On the African plains, robo-cameras have been covered in elephant dung or disguised as rocks or trees. The animals around them were curious at first, as the robo-cams moved on their wheels and whirred, but they gradually took less notice. Other robo-cams recorded a family of tigers as the mother hunted prey to feed her growing cubs.

Underwater Robots

There are many kinds of robotic fish and other water creatures. Robotuna is designed to study how fish swim. Robocarp can hide in a big pond or lake containing valuable koi and similar fish, and photograph fish-nappers who try to steal them. Other robot fish take water samples and **analyze** them. ESP, the Environmental Sample Processor, is a whole underwater robot laboratory. It tests water samples for DNA and other substances from living things, to find out what lives in the area.

ROBO-FUTURE

Takeoff

Most robots are quite heavy—but not Robo-bird. It is incredibly lightweight and one of the few machines to fly by flapping rather than using a propeller or jet engine. Robo-bird has solar panels on its wings, and one day it may fly among bird flocks to film and study them, or soar unsuspected on spying missions over enemy territory.

▼ *A robo-cam disguised as a rock can record white rhinos relaxing. This would be a dangerous task for a human photographer, as rhinos can charge without warning!*

Doctor Robots

"Hello there, please sit down. What seems to be the trouble? Beep-beep, whirr." The opportunity to visit a robot doctor rather than a human one is a long way off. But robots of many kinds are used in medicine to keep us healthy and treat our illnesses.

Out of Sight

Many of the robots in medicine are behind the scenes. They are used by staff and health workers, but never seen by patients. In hospital medical stores, they check the stocks and count out every patient's pills for the nurses to take around the wards. In medical laboratories, rows of robot machines analyze samples of blood, saliva (spit), and other substances, for germs and other problems. So when the doctor tells a patient, "Your tests are all clear," several robots have been involved in carrying out those tests.

◄◄ *Robots automatically fetch and carry medical supplies, such as pills, tubes, and bandages, by following wires buried under the floor.*

Robots in Action ■

HEALTH CHECKS

Each year, health equipment becomes more automatic and robot-like. Machines take a person's temperature, pulse rate and blood pressure, and listen to the heart and lungs. They measure weight and height, and ask questions on a computer screen about a person's food, lifestyle, and exercise. Often people give more honest answers to a robot machine than to a human doctor. ■

DO YOU KNOW?

(ROBOTS DO)

Data Risk

*There is a chance that any kind of robot memory system or **database** could break down. This could be a real problem in medicine, where a patient's records must be kept private or confidential. A robot memory breakdown might result in lost data or information going to the wrong people.*

On the Ward

In some hospitals, a doctor might be a robot—or at least a real doctor on a monitor screen. The screen is mounted on a robot that tours hospital wards. It has cameras, a speaker, and a microphone, so the doctor can see and talk to patients, and they can ask the doctor questions. Patients usually say they are comforted by seeing their doctor face to face.

These robots allow doctors to interact with their patients from far away. Army doctors can talk with injured troops overseas. In small rural hospitals, patients can talk to a specialist without having to travel to a large city. Being able to see the patients can help doctors give better care than they could over the phone.

▶▶ *The doctor controls this roving robot from his office, steering it around wards so he can see and chat with patients.*

Toward a Robo-body

The first artificial body parts were made thousands of years ago, which included wooden teeth and toes and metal noses. Today there are all kinds of intelligent artificial parts that can sense, move, decide, and react, to help their owner live a better life. Could people in the future be **cyborgs**—combinations of human parts and robot machinery?

▼ *This artificial hand is controlled by sensors that detect tightening or flexing of the living muscles at the end of the arm.*

More Every Week

The list of robotic body parts, or **prostheses**, grows longer almost every week. There are artificial electric-powered arms and hands. There is also electronic skin, which is as sensitive to touch as ordinary human skin. Robotic legs move under battery power to help the wearer walk and even run. Intelligent **pacemakers** can be implanted under the skin near the heart to help it beat regularly, and speed up or slow down according to the body's needs. Some of the most exciting developments are robotic aids that allow blind people to see and deaf people to hear.

ROBO-FUTURE

Helping Hands

Artificial hands and legs are improving all the time. Wearers activate muscles under the skin near them, and sensor pads on the skin pick up the signals to feed to the hand and make it move. One day sensors implanted into the brain could send radio signals to the hand, so the wearer just has to think and it moves.

Retinal implants go into the light-sensitive retina inside the eyeball to help with vision. **Cochlear implants** are put into the inner ear, where they change sound vibrations into nerve signals for the brain.

Cry Baby

Robot patients can be very useful for training student doctors and nurses. BabySIM is a robot baby that cries, drools, has a pulse, makes baby noises, and even "dies" if a medical student makes a mistake. PediaSIM is the child version. You can listen to its breathing and heartbeat, see its eyes blink, and watch the eye pupils react to light. It also pees—but it doesn't throw temper tantrums!

ROBOT OR NOT?
○○○

Learning Limbs

Aids such as the Rheo knee are artificial-intelligence robotic joints. They do not just swing to and fro. They pick up their user's habits and learn to fit in with them, so the person moves more naturally. These are robots rather than simple artificial aids.

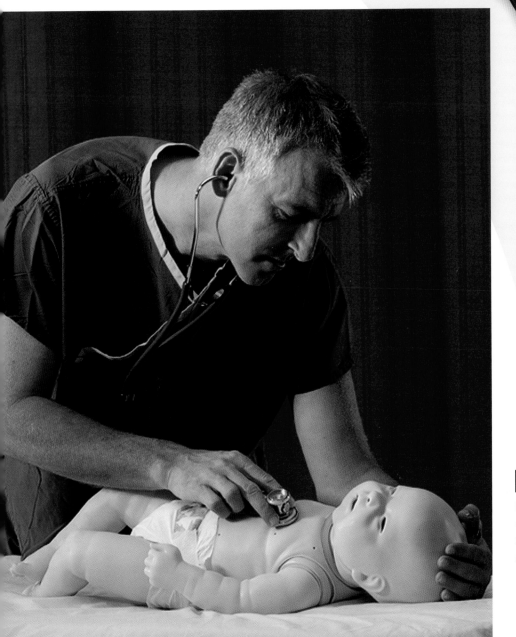

◄◄ *Babies react differently than adults when they have certain illnesses. Doctors can find out how by training on BabySIM.*

21

Surgery by Robots

An expert surgeon needs a steady hand, a delicate grip, precise movements, good eyesight, and a massive memory for body parts and operation methods. Scientists have built robot surgeons with all these qualities to be able to do even more precise surgeries.

ROBOT SUPERSTAR

Da Vinci

*One of the main robot surgery set-ups is da Vinci. Every day surgeons around the world use it to carry out more than 100 operations on patients, including inserting new heart **valves**, mending stomachs, and removing diseased pieces of intestine.*

Surgeon Far Away

When a tricky operation has to be done, and no one on site has experience with doing it, a **surgeon** who's an expert can carry it out from thousands of miles away! This is remote surgery or **telesurgery**.

One remote surgery method allows the surgeon to move handles and levers at a remote operating station. As these move, information is sent through the communications network (just like the Internet) to control the mechanical arms, pincers, blades, grabs, suckers, and other surgical tools next to the patient miles away.

Several cameras view the patient from different angles so the remote surgeon can watch the operation live on TV screens. The cameras can zoom in to give a magnified view of body parts smaller than this letter "o." The surgeon's movements are scaled down or reduced so the remote tool movements are incredibly tiny and accurate. This is known as **microsurgery**. Meanwhile, assistants and nurses look after the patient, equipment, breathing tubes, and IVs.

Pretend Patients

Robot patients are used to train surgeons. The handles and levers at the operating station control a virtual scene where saws, blades, forceps (tweezers), and other surgical tools cut into a simulated (imaginary) patient shown on a screen. The robot's memory allows surgeons to operate on the patient just as if it were a real person. One benefit is that a slip of the scalpel won't hurt anyone!

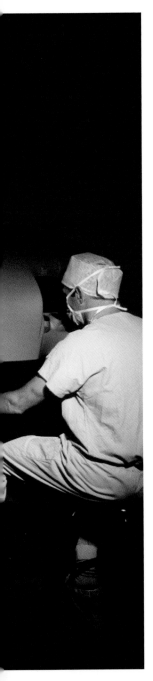

ROBO-FUTURE

Saving Soldiers' Lives

Soldiers can suffer terrible injuries in war and often need emergency surgery. Army doctors at a battlefield cannot be experts in everything. One day, army medical centers at battlefields may have a robot surgery setup. That would allow a large team of experts back at base to carry out all kinds of operations at the front line.

◀◀ *The da Vinci robot surgeon (in clear plastic) operates on a real patient, but not by itself. It's controlled by the human surgeon sitting at the console on the right, who views the scene on close-up screens.*

▶▶ *Penelope the robot nurse unpacks operating instruments, such as scalpels, arranges them on the tray, and hands them to the surgeon when they're needed.*

cameras

robotic arm

magnet

Robot Helpers

Medical problems can make everyday life difficult. Some people find it hard to move around easily, cook, or bathe. Robots to the rescue! More and more robotic aids are helping people enjoy a better quality of life.

Back to Reality

Robotic aids are a great help to people who are ill or have medical problems. But could people come to depend too much on their mechanical friends? It's tricky to know when robots should be replaced with real pets, real people, and real life.

Wakamaru is a 3 foot (1 m) tall home companion. It recognizes thousands of words, obeys commands, and can chat in a simple way.

▶▶ *Robotic Robina is powered by electric motors, with sensors to detect obstructions in case its driver does not. Many routes can be programmed into its memory, giving a smooth ride even over rough ground.*

Robo-chairs

The latest robotic wheelchairs are a great advance on older versions. They are powered by electric motors and have cameras that scan each room, as well as a computer to store the memory map. The wheelchairs also respond to voice commands. So if the user says, "Take me to the kitchen," the chair can safely find its own way around obstacles to the right place.

Cheered Up

Being stuck at home can lead to problems such as depression. Robot makers have produced several human-shaped home helpers and companions. These can do simple jobs, such as fetching and carrying, and they also respond to a voice and speak. They might describe what's on TV or report the latest news using information they receive over a **wifi** link from the Internet. This helps to pass the time and entertain people who can't leave their homes.

Another way to improve quality of life is to own a pet. If a real pet presents problems, there are robot pets which are much more than toys. Robot puppies, kittens, a baby seal, and even a baby dinosaur can make people feel happier and more wanted.

Robots in Action■

A NEW PET

Paro the cuddly seal pup is one of several types of robot friends and companions. Paro blinks and wags its tail when stroked and even shows emotions such as happiness and sadness. Paro's owner can teach the baby seal to recognize and respond to various words, just like training a real pet.■

Can Robots Have Feelings?

Robots are good at physical tasks and practical jobs such as carrying and lifting. But how well do they perform mental tasks? Should advanced robots have feelings and emotions so that they can become angry or cry with happiness?

Androids

Robots built to resemble humans, with a body, head, and face, are known as androids. The most advanced androids look so human, and move in such a human way, that they can fool us for a few moments. These are highly specialized robots, built for research or to show off their makers' skills. They are not really for everyday use—at least, not yet.

Making Faces

If robots had feelings, how would they show them? Smiles, frowns, and other facial expressions are very important. They show us what other people are thinking. If a robot has no face for us to look at, this makes us react differently to it, with less emotion.

◀◀ *Under the skin of a robot that makes facial expressions are many levers, motors, gears, pulleys, and other parts.*

ROBOT SUPERSTAR

Data the Android

The mega-hit series Star Trek: The Next Generation *features the **android** Data. He is a human-like android with amazing intelligence, one of the staff on the starship* Enterprise. *But Data cannot understand human feelings, so people's behavior often puzzles him. In some episodes he has an "emotion chip"—an electronic microchip that gives him feelings. But this makes him too emotional and he gets into trouble.*

Several teams of robot researchers are giving their robots human-like faces to show expressions. Most of these faces have a rubber mask with electric motors, or **actuators**, behind it, to move areas of the skin in, out, or sideways. Some face robots can respond to spoken words. If you say "fear," the face looks frightened. In their research, the scientists study the faces of the people who are watching the robot faces.

The actor-robot Actroid DER-2 (on the right) moves its arms and hands, smiles, frowns, laughs, and talks. It can be programmed to sing, make a speech, or welcome guests.

ROBO-FUTURE

Ups and Downs?

If advanced robots had emotional ups and downs, would this help? Usually we want robots simply to obey our instructions. If they started to sulk or complain or sing with joy, we might not want them at all.

Created by Hanson Robotics in the U.S., Joey Chaos has "attitude." The robot recognizes many spoken words, and loves to tell you its thoughts and opinions —even if you don't want to hear them! The spongy, smooth, stretchy skin is moved by small electric motors called servos.

A Nanobot Revolution

Nano means far smaller than micro—it's about as tiny as you can get. So nano-robots are the smallest robots possible. You could fit 100 of them on the dot of this letter "i." But what use are they?

Tiny but Helpful

The science of incredibly small things is called **nanotechnology**. This branch of science is big, moving fast, and going places—and it has robots. One of the most exciting areas for nanotechnology in the future is medical **nanobots**. Thousands of them could be put into a body with one small injection. They could be designed to carry out tasks such as taking a medical drug to the body part where it is needed and then releasing the drug. This would mean that other parts of the body would not be affected by the drug, and could cut down on any side effects caused by the drug.

Medical nanobots might also dissolve troublesome blood clots such as those that cause heart attacks and strokes. They could mend damaged nerves, which is a very difficult task using today's technology.

▼ *In this imaginary future scene, nanobots mend a microscopic, spider-like nerve cell in the brain. This could help people think faster and remember more.*

Nano Army

Small ants work together in colonies to build huge nests and overpower much bigger animals. In the same way, it would take millions of nanobots working together to complete large jobs. But what would happen if we couldn't control nanobots?

Small 'Bots, Big Work

Nanobots might do many other jobs in the wider world, especially where chemicals are involved. They are so small that they could go in among **chemical particles** and change them. Nanobots might clear up oil spills at sea, clean up a polluted river, and make dirty soil safe for wildlife. Of course you would need millions, or even billions, of them, so some nanobots could be designed to make other nanobots in micro-factories. However, some people worry that humans wouldn't be able to control nanobots if we can't see them.

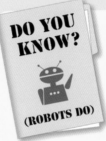

DO YOU KNOW?

(ROBOTS DO)

Hidden Menace?

One problem with nanobots is that they are so tiny we cannot see them. If a few were to escape, we would not know. They could multiply unseen, until they were so widespread and numerous that they were like germs, ready to cause disease and death.

▶▶ *Thick, sticky spilled oil kills fish, birds, and other sea life. One day, pouring a few buckets full of oil-dispersing nanobots into the water could make the black slime melt away.*

Glossary

actuator
A device that produces controlled movements or actions, such as an electric motor, or a lever worked by hydraulics.

AI (artificial intelligence)
Intelligence or cleverness in a machine rather than in a living person. This includes knowing what is happening around it, making decisions, and taking actions that help it survive and carry out tasks.

algorithms
Step-by-step sets of instructions for solving a problem or changing one type of information into another, for example, changing sound waves into computer mp3 files.

analyze
To study something and find out what is in it or how it works.

android
A robot or similar machine designed to resemble a human, usually with a face, arms, body, and legs.

automatic
A series of actions or events that happens by itself, without human help.

CCD
Stands for charge-coupled device, a special kind of microchip that changes patterns of light rays from the scene it "sees" into similar patterns of electrical signals for a computer.

chemical particles
The tiniest pieces or molecules of a particular substance or material, which are far too small to see.

circuit
In electrical equipment, the path or route of electricity through various wires, switches, microchips, and other parts.

cochlear implant
A microchip put into the cochlea deep inside the ear, to change sound waves into electrical signals.

cyborg
Something that is partly living and partly machinery, with mechanical, electronic, and similar devices. Usually one part cannot exist without the other. (There are no true cyborgs as of yet.)

database
Lots of information or data, organized so it is easy to find specific parts of it.

decibels
A measure of the loudness or volume of sounds, from a quiet whisper at 10 dB to a rocket blasting off at 150 dB.

digital
Working by numbers, especially the two numbers 1 and 0—that is, an electrical signal and no electrical signal—as used in digital equipment such as computers.

electronics
Machines that work by very small signals or pulses of electricity.

formulas
Types of sums or math that give the answer to a problem from a set of information.

hydraulic system
A system powered by a liquid under pressure, such as oil or water, pumped into a pipe that creates a pushing force at the other end.

infrared light
Light with waves slightly longer than red light waves. Human eyes cannot see infrared light, but some animals' eyes can.

microchip
A small, flat piece of a substance such as silicon, with thousands of microscopic electronic parts on its surface.

microsurgery
Using microscopes, micro-blades, and similar very small instruments to mend a tiny part of the body, such as a hair-thin nerve.

nanobot
A robot of nano size, which is smaller than micro size, measured in billionths of a meter.

nanotechnology
The science of machines and devices that measure just a few billionths of a meter, which is the same as millionths of a millimeter. This is the scale of the tiniest pieces of substances, called atoms and molecules.

pacemaker
An electrical device put into the body and attached to the heart by a wire, to keep it beating in a healthy way.

pressure pads
Small pads with switches inside that detect pressure or touch and produce electrical signals.

prosthesis
A non-natural or man-made body part, ranging from a false tooth to a plastic heart valve, mechanical hand, or artificial joint.

retinal implant
A microchip put into the retina inside the rear of the eyeball, to change light waves into electrical signals.

robotics
The science of robots, how they are designed and made, and the jobs and work they can do.

sensor
A device that detects something, such as light, sound, touch, heat, or certain chemicals.

silicon
A natural, pure substance used to make microchips and other electronic devices.

surgeon
A doctor who specializes in carrying out operations, cutting and moving and mending body parts to treat illness and cure disease.

telesurgery
Carrying out surgery at a distance, usually with the surgeon in one place controlling robot arms and other devices at the patient's side somewhere else.

ultraviolet light
Light with waves slightly shorter than violet light waves. Human eyes cannot see ultraviolet light, but some animals' eyes can.

valve
A part that controls the flow or movement of something, such as a liquid, gas, or powder. Sink faucets are a type of valve.

wifi
Wireless devices or machines that work together using invisible radio waves rather than electrical wires.

Further Reading

Davis, Barbara. *The Kids' Guide to Robots.* Kids' Guides. Mankato, Minn: Capstone Press, 2010.

Hyland, Tony. *Scientific and Medical Robots.* Robots and Robotics. Mankato, Minn.: Smart Apple Media, 2008.

Jefferis, David. *Robot Brains.* Robozones. New York: Crabtree Publishing, 2007.

Strom, Laura Layton. *From Bugbots to Humanoids: Robotics.* Shockwave. New York : Children's Press, 2008.

Van Voorst, Jennifer. *Rise of the Thinking Machines: The Science of Robots.* Headline Science. Minneapolis: Compass Point Books, 2008.

Web Sites

Elbot
Visit with this online "robot" who was programmed to carry on intelligent conversations with people. His programmer won the Loebner Prize for Artifical Intelligence in 2008.
http://www.elbot.com/

Lego Mindstorms NXT
Learn how to build your own robot with a Lego Mindstorms robotic kit and talk to robotic experts.
http://mindstorms.lego.com

Robot World News
This site covers the top news stories on robotics, artificial intelligence and related areas, but it also has more fun information on robots such as toys.
http://www.robotworldnews.com/robots4u.html

Robot Video Clips
Video clips of all kinds of robots in action.
http://www.robotclips.com/

Index

store

DATE DUE

FEB 2 4 2001		
MAY 2 0 2002		
JUN - 3 2002		
GAYLORD		PRINTED IN U.S.A.